Partick Remembered

by

Bill Spalding

The Western cinema was originally known as the Garrick when it opened in the 1920s on the site of the old Gas Works, later the location of Avery's weighing-machine works. Judging by the queue, the cinema was enjoying Saturday's regular 'penny crush'. Just beyond the cinema, on the corner of Benalder Street, is the Old Masonic Bar, now the Partick Tavern and the chimney of the Partick Pumping Station rises in the distance. The cinema has since been demolished and the site has remained unused for several years.

Allan's, established in 1887, supplied a remarkably large range of services for such a small shop. Not only a news-agent's, the shop was also a lending library and dealt with printing, lithography, bookbinding and frame-making as well as stocking artists' materials. The plate at the bottom of the door bears the well-remembered advertising slogan, - "They come as a boon and a blessing to men, the Pickwick, the Owl and the Waverley Pen." To the left is the old entrance to Partick Hill station, and the shops have been replaced by Woolworth's.

FOREWORD

My two earlier books, *Bygone Partick* and *Bygone Partick 2*, showed Partick as it looked between 1900 and 1912 - the area's last years as a burgh. This volume covers Partick's first forty years as a district of the City of Glasgow and gives an indication of the rapid acceleration of change during those years which took the district far beyond its village days.

Nevertheless, by the 1950s much of the old Partick still existed along with the new, a situation not only evident in the wealth of Art Deco shop facades from the '30s and '40s standing alongside earlier exteriors, but also in the continuation of traditional tenement life shown here.

Bill Spalding,
26 Lamington Road, Cardonald,
Glasgow, G52 2SE,
February 1995

An anonymous bakery undergoes a refit.

The Windsor Bar is now no more. Next door, the Rosevale Cinema became a bingo hall, then a billiard club and is now a supermarket. The young lad posing nonchalantly for the photographer is leaning on a set of still photos from the film being shown - *Other People's Sins*.

4

Fresh supplies being delivered to the Windsor.

The fruit shop at 340 Dumbarton Road had a southern exposure, hence the lowered blind to keep the sun off the produce. However, the cat seems to be enjoying it.

Partick West, 1939. A typical pawn shop with the three brass balls in a prominent corner position, windows on the main road and the entrance in the side street - Sawmill Road. Men's suits hang outside the windows for passengers on the upper deck of the trams to see. The van's license plate has the letters US for Govan - in 1903 these, along with YS for Partick, were among the first registration letters to be issued in Britain. This building was demolished when the Expressway was formed.

Tramcar on Dumbarton Road, looking west from the N.B. railway bridge.

Woman newspaper-vendor at the corner of Rosevale Street. A commissionaire stands at the doorway of the Rosevale Bar behind and in the distance is the N.B. railway bridge.

Tram stop at Hayburn Vaults, 1920s. The public convenience situated under the Robin advert is now closed and has been relocated at the corner of Peel Street and Burgh Hall Street.

A fine view of the popular gents outfitters at the corner of Hayburn Street. James Hoey had been established in Castle Street for some years before opening a shop in Dumbarton Road around 1918. In 1926 the company expanded by taking over the ladies clothes shop on the corner and became D.M. Hoey Ltd. The business began in 1886 when Samuel Hoey set up shop in Springburn Road and it is still a family-run business.

In the old days no man would have been seen dead in charge of a pram, but by the '50s attitudes were changing. The men are probably standing outside Hoey's.

Partick pre-nuptials, 1955. Here a prospective bride and groom suffer an exercise in embarrassment normally reserved for the female of the couple. Normally, the happy bride-to-be was dragged through the streets in outlandish clothes, her friends making as much noise as possible and collecting donations for the couple in a chanty (chamber pot). Here, however, the groom unusually shares in the mortification.

A little-known path in Partick; Hayburn Lane which is just south of Dudley Drive on the border of the old burgh. The same type of business is still carried on here. The building on the right is the signal box at Partick Junction on the Stobcross Line of the N.B. Railway. The tenements of Thornwood are in the distance.

The vast bulk of the Granary looms above this yard in Meadow Road. There have been ice cream shops in Partick since at least the early 1900s, virtually all owned by Italians. E. De Marco's ice cream vans, garaged at this yard, probably toured housing schemes, such as Knightswood and Drumchapel. In the centre of the picture at the side of the Granary, can be seen the name 'Codona's', the people who brought the 'shows' to the Kelvin Hall and elsewhere in Glasgow. They mostly wintered in various sites in Partick - latterly on the vacant site of Barclay, Curle in Whiteinch.

The Western Bar at the foot of Peel Street no longer exits, the attractive invitation to 'Happy Days' with Regalia Highland Whisky long gone with it.

A soap-box orator from the Hillhead Labour Party holds forth at the foot of Peel Street - a long established site for those claiming to know how to right the wrongs of this world. The flag-poles in the top right of the picture are still there.

These two workmen passing the bank at the western corner of Peel Street appear to be slaters. The slow-moving midden lorry has probably come up from the Cleansing Depot in Sandy Road. On the pole alongside the midden lorry there is a fire alarm with a replica of a fireman's helmet at the top. After breaking the glass in the centre, one pushed a knob which rang a bell in the nearest fire station - at Sandy Road.

The coal rees at Partick Central Station as seen from Benalder Street. By the '50s other fuels had been added to the stocks of coal.

The Standard Picture House was built some time after the end of World War I, and its entrance was down the pend on the left. Later, the low building in the middle of the picture was taken down and a white extension built as an entrance to the Standard. The notice above the pend, "Patrons can follow their pictures at the Star Palace, Partick", was an invitation to the F & F, a little further west along Dumbarton Road.

The F & F Palais de Danse started life as the Olympia Roller Rink, before becoming the Star Picture Palace and Theatre of Varieties. It was showing films by July 1910 and by the 1930s it offered dancing three days a week and roller skating on three others. There was a Sunday cafe with orchestral music too. These musical events continued during the war, and amateur singers who fancied their chances could get up and perform during the 'go-as-you-please'. These buildings are still standing today.

The National Bank of Scotland at the corner of Dumbarton Road and Stewartville Street. The latter street follows the line of one of two tree-lined avenues, which in village days led up to a mansion house called Stewart Ville.

Here we are in South Street close to the western boundary of the burgh. The lines are not tramlines but the tracks of the Whiteinch Branch Railway. Steam locomotives ran along South Street and Scotstoun Street with tracks running into various firms, including Barclay, Curle's. On the left can be seen one of the bridges carrying the Lanarkshire & Dumbartonshire lines of the Caledonian Railway. That line was closed down in 1965 and the section between Meadowside and Balloch has been transformed into part of the cycleway from Glasgow to Loch Lomond.

The steamie in Purdon Street, built in 1912 on a site which had previously held sheds and a stable. Scrubbing boards had a space at the top to hold a bar of Sunlight Soap. Tin baths and wicker baskets, or even better an old pram, were used for carrying washing in. Water in the stalls was piping hot, and the machines at the front were also available for use, although at extra cost.

Even by the '50s a dustman's was a filthy and exhausting job. The midden-man had to shovel all the refuse, which before the smoke-free zone consisted very largely of ashes and dust, into his wicker basket, humph this onto his shoulders, carry it up the back stairs, through the close and over to the midden lorry waiting in the street.

As well as providing facilities for washing clothes and hanging them out to dry, backcourts could also be used for partying, an indulgence for all ages.

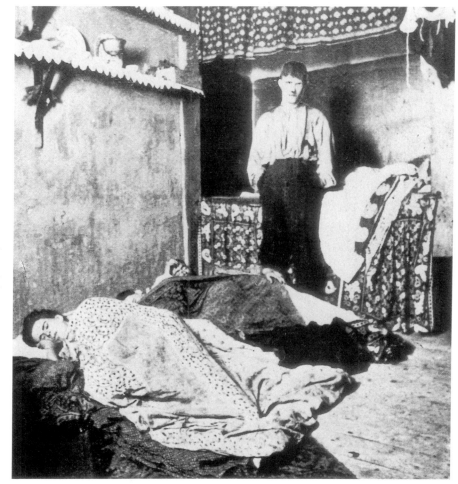

A Ticketed House. So-called because a ticket, a small oval-shaped metal plate with a number, was fixed to the front door. The number referred to the maximum number of people allowed by law to live in that house - a half referred to a child under eight years of age. This was done after the smallpox epidemic of 1872, and by 1914 about 10% of Glasgow's housing was ticketed. It was an attempt to prevent overcrowding, as not only was accommodation in demand, but tenants took in lodgers to help pay the rent. In Partick these were affixed to houses south of Dumbarton Road, the oldest of the tenements. These tickets were still in place during the Second World War. The date of this photograph is unknown but the poverty is obvious.

The Victoria Bar. Anderson Street is reflected in the left-hand window.

After this extensive shop-fitting job, the shop became a branch of Munro the Butchers. Note that the windows in the pawn shop above have been strengthened. This building has now been demolished entirely and replaced with an open leisure site.

The couple are crossing over Crawford Street. The first tenement on the right was demolished when Rosevale Street was aligned with Crow Road to facilitate the movement of traffic. New low housing has been built here and Crawford Street, which used to run north to south, now runs through them from east to west. The canopy of the Rosevale Cinema can be seen in the distance.

This discreet wallpaper shop, situated at the south side of Partick Cross, was once a pawnshop. The building has now been demolished and the site is vacant. To the left is Partick Bridge Street and to the right, Cooperswell Street, both dating back to the early days of Partick village.

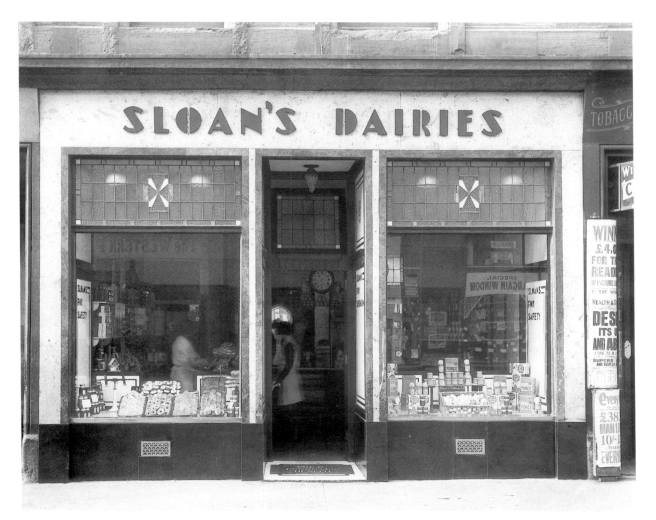

Andrew Sloan, an Ayrshire farmer, began his dairy business in 1911. His shop in Merkland Street has only ever closed once, in 1980 when the subway was being modernised. The scales on the left of the right-hand window were made by Avery, a Partick firm.

De Simone's cafe in Merkland Street, where, despite the classy exterior, you could still get traditional Glasgow favourites like hot peas and vinegar.

A very up-to-date looking chemist shop. Note the somewhat unusual and expensive name plate.

The Barber's beneath the pawnshop in Merkland Street. Harry Hood's premises next door appear to be a garage from which deliveries were made. Long established in Partick, Hood's main shop was around the corner in Dumbarton Road.

Another business bites the dust to make way for modernisation. The little plate in the close belongs to Alex Bridges, Dentist, who occupied the first floor flat on the corner of Crow Road above the bank.

Bell's and R.S. McColl now occupy the premises with a shared entrance and a facade which outshines those of the fish shop and the chemist.

Dead dog disaster at Miller's Corner. Miller's hardware store later moved up Hyndland Street to the corner of Chancellor Street and the above site is now occupied by the Quarter Gill public house.

A Partick flood, December 1956.

The facade of Price's and the elegant fur of the lady standing in the close are both typical of the 1930s.

An evangelist from Abingdon Hall in nearby Stewartville Street holds an open-air meeting at the top of Merkland Street. At the right-hand corner is the entrance to the City Bakeries. Half-way down on the left is the back exit of the New Partick Picture House. The old Partick Picture House was the first cinema built in Partick, and used to be on the same site. Built in 1912, it was destroyed by fire in the 1920s.

This branch of Boots the Chemists has a smart '30s facade. A decorative glass plate in a first storey window says "Branch of the Cottage Nurses Home Govan", a subsidiary branch of the Elder Cottage Hospital in Govan.

More very attractive Art Deco frontages. On the right we also have a tiled or 'wally' close. The more tiles in the close and the more decorative they were, the higher the class of the occupants.

A delivery to the butcher's at 566 Dumbarton Road. With few homes having telephones in the first half of this century, the blue signs such as the one on the immediate right were commonly seen outside newsagents. The bridge in the distance is the more easterly of the two bridges at Partick West Station.

The defunct Cafe Royal with Subway Lane on the left. The premises with the door at the end of the lane (The Fleet Deliveries Ltd) were converted to a little newspaper kiosk by the 1950s. Robertson's butchers was established in 1810.

A view looking east to Partick Cross. Fairbanks Menswear, on the left, used to be the Strand Cafe and is now a charity shop. Next door is the entrance to Partick Cross subway station, now called Kelvinhall. Above the entrance is the sign for Hall the stationers, whose premises were on the ground floor of the Subway Halls. Then comes the large and popular Walker's of Partick which sold ladies' clothing. Next is Price's the bakers, Marshall's shoe shop and another shop before Bayne & Ducket's shoe shop at the corner of Byres Road. George Ducket lived in Partickhill.

Looking west towards Partick Cross. The only changes that have been made to these buildings is that they have now been stone-cleaned, although the shops have nearly all changed ownership and purpose. Next to the bank at the corner of Byres Road is Templeton's newsagents which distributed the Evening Times and the Evening News to other local newsagents before the shop was closed and used to extend the bank. Evening Citizens were collected from a newsagent's facing Templeton's. Besides other women's clothing, Kelvin House (still trading today) stocked uniforms worn by the nurses at the nearby Western Infirmary.

The rear of a three-storied tenement in Thornwood. Behind stands Crathie Court, designed in 1946 and built in 1952-4. It is a U-shaped block of six to eight storeys with 88 single-person flats with balcony access. The building won the Saltire Award for the best-designed Scottish flats of 1952.